A time to PLANT and a time to REAP

**A Poetic Commentary on the substance
of life from the Trivial to the Cataclysmic.**

by

MARGOT REICH

A time to PLANT and a time to REAP

ISBN 978-0-9552404-6-1

Published by

i2i Publishing. Manchester M8 5DT. UK

www.i2ipublishing.co.uk

Dedications:

My Special Thanks to Marina who typed my poems to see the first light of day.

My gratitude to Benno (Ben) for his constant compliments. They made me feel humbled.

My appreciation to Nitza Spiro for her unstinted praise at all times

'Nothing is possible without faith'

United We Stand

Strange or not, common experience
changes people,
Entering a synagogue for high service as
individuals,
Very much their own kind,
They are transformed into a unit,
Like individual cadets become a cohesive
group after training,
Prayers have that impact,
The atmosphere changes, as if standing
on shifting ground,
The ground becomes firm,
A safe landing,
Enveloped in its transformation,
It regularly happens, without fail,
The feeling is very special,
Uplifting of the spirit to a corporate
body,
At one with God and the world.

Chanting in unity to proclaim God's
unity,
Not for our own appraisal,

Confirming God's glory only as if angels
are also joining,
Like a huge orchestration of a basic
concept,
Feelings of disembodiment almost
overcomes one, ethereal, surreal,
Living not on this earth, but between
heaven and earth.

Having fasted the whole day,
Where does the strength come from?
To pronounce basic principles with such
fervour.

Possessed by a Dybuck,
The whole human being is invaded
totally,
As if cast by a spell,
It is a good time to start anew,
Feeling elated and privileged and
optimistic,
'With God's help we proclaim into a new
year.'

God

We, who question, waiting for miracles,

Answers –

They never come.

And yet always requesting, searching,

Till eternity ends.

If there is a God – there the scale ends.

Has He got requests?

Is He pleased with His imperfections?

Who answers His doubts and worries?

Does He listen?

Does He reflect?

Was He satisfied on the eighth day?

Jerusalem

The sun is not of this world,
The wind is not of this world,
The rain is not of this world,
The atmosphere is not of this world,
The people are not of this mould,
They are different from the rest,
Handcrafted with a fine chisel, not a
hammer,
Painted with a pointed brush, a rare
substance,
Holiness is not the word.

People are drawn to live in God's frame,
Recognisable without a passport, like
halos covering their heads,
Like tefillin on their foreheads,
City imbued with years of yearning,
Surviving, only just, holding their own
against the odds,
God has not deserted His sanctuary,
Despite provocations of one kind or
another.

The circumference of His wings,

Blesses and colours surroundings,
For those who believe in ancient
prophecy yesterday,
To be renewed as before, from generation
to generation,
As it was said.

The bricks have looked into the deepest
of hearts,
Witnessing and sharing the innermost
secrets like members of a jury,
Sworn to secrecy,
Not revealing anything, locked up in
themselves,
And to the world.

Gateway to Heaven

Waves lapping against the sea wall,

Disrupting the tranquillity of time,

Spoiling the effect of peace,

The ships establish their own ripple
patterns,

Facilitating a gateway to heaven.

Break

Loosen the reins,
Release the brakes,
Untie the laces,
Give the pulse a new tempo.

Time for recharging,
Let new sap flow,
Unstoppable, cascading,
Like a waterfall in mountain terrain,
New-found spring of life.

The boughs bend and break,
Carrying their own offspring,
Under pressure everything weakens,
Except faith which carries a flame, burns
brighter.

The Wall

How many tears will sustain those
ancient bricks?
Will trees find sustenance in their
crevices?
They are only just sprouting a green
growth of weeds.

Nothing grows without nourishment,
Will the broken veined stones change
and bring forth thorns and thistles?

It's an old melody that repeats over the
wall,
Years and centuries have not changed the
refrain,
It has all been heard before,
They already know what is coming.

Do they still listen and become bored?
Answers are requested,
Deeds are required to calm stormy hearts
and change history,
Or is it all in vain?

It is still the same God of old,
Enveloped in the same garment of
yesterday,

Mail must be answered, a letter without
an address,
He knows it all, words are no substitute.

It's a full-time job,
Acknowledging every request,
His work schedule is demanding,
Only overtime can cope with such a load,
Without an end in sight.

Nothing is possible without faith,
Despair can be cast out,
Or re-channelled in their tunnelled
location.

Multitudes gather only to pray and
plead,
To be heard in the midst of tears,
The tears cut out the prayer and wailing,
To be rekindled again,
Like a fire, to be consumed again.

'I hear what you say' – is the well-
rehearsed reply,
We wait to hear you utter those words,
In such a very quiet and private arena,
yet turbulent open place.

<u>By Association</u>

We carry fate on our shoulders,
It is a burden,
Oh God, to escape destiny for once.

To be weightless like in space,
Just to float,
We are different since our wanderings,
Journeys inevitably come to an end,
The luggage is better distributed now,
We carry it more lightly,
Lest we become unbalanced.

Like the ox who carried his yoke for
generations,
To unburden oneself,
Only to miss the burden itself,
It is tougher than the known pressure
points.

<u>Your Smile</u>

Your radiating smile sets the world
alight,
Reaching corners, penetrating crevices,
However hidden, elucidating immediate
response.

Who cannot be charmed by such rays?
It does not burn; it has its own intensity,
Casting spells all around,
Gripping bystanders and spectators
alike,
Forever indebted for your magic.

For you are no magician,
Practicing your skill like a juggler,
You are not conscious of your magnetic
effect,
Your power envelopes everything, like a
tallis,
Not unlike tentacles gripping all within
reach.

'Testing Times'

J' accuse

Can damage be assessed?
Can you imagine the unimaginable?

Killing Jews is just a sentence,
Signifying not much.

By killing Jews you killed our guardians
and protectors.
You robbed me of treasures untold,
My innocence, my childhood.

You robbed me of trust in humanity,
By making us outcasts, not part of this
planet,
'Vermin' at the beginning and at the end.

God was nowhere to be heard or seen,
Hiding away during testing times.

You robbed us of time to blossom and
grow,
We learnt slowly and quickly,
Making good, making up.

Cost in turmoil and despair,

You even killed hope,
But not forever.

Not all flames can be extinguished,
Salvaging leftovers, trying to build
On shaking foundations.

Yet we all surfaced,
Hope appears in small packages.
High ambitions did not materialise.

Our lost families would be proud of us,
We made new lives out of grains of
ashes,
Broken vessels were salvages with
broken remnants,
Of little worth to bystanders.

You sinned against humanity,
You sinned against God and His
creation,
And almost succeeded.

Forgiving is out of the question,
Forgetting an impossibility – not just for
me,
But for generations that follow.

<u>On Collision Course</u>

The ancient, past, present,
Abounded like a knitted twin set,
Taking from one, adding to another,
Making new balance sheets like old trees,
with intertwined branches,
Or ancient menorot, with twisted arms
linked or locked together,
When branches break, connections are
broken.

Repairs are not easy,
Where do we stand? Are the roots rooted
in fertile soil?
And foundations solid with secure
scaffolding into long nights?
New grafting on old shoulders. Old
shoulders stretch out for support,
Completing a perfect circle in a square
network, with variegated leaves.

A Fishy Tale

My cooked carp is legendary.
Observing multitudes in a tiny bath,
Gasping for air, in captivity,
Fighting to catch their breath.
Suffocating to death and more.

I vowed never to be a consumer again.

That, eating my words and them,
Savouring the flavour,
A recurring dilemma.

<u>Henry Moore</u>

Holes filled to the brim,
Encapsulating a vacuum,
Like meaningful, pregnant pauses.

Eyes can be fooled,
Imagination does the rest,
What there is – is not,
What is not – is there,
Strange, yet completely real and true.

Deception – makes sense,
Holes – become full circles,
All becomes clean like a clean window
without smudges.

Like mist and fog early at dawn,
It all falls into place,
The mysterious is no longer a mystery,
His skeletal bones are unclad,
Yet they radiate warmth from within,
No veins and arteries are to be seen,
Yet blood is pulsating at a regular rate.

The setting provides air and breath and
sanity,
Ready for take-off to another location,
The stones are solid and contented.

Not looking for other destinations,
Blending into the world harmoniously,
Having long ago given up the search,
They are well placed and settled.

Unlike the restless wandering Jew,
displaced, unsettled.
Still on the lookout,
Moving on and on for a suitable place to
pause,
To hang up his boots for repair,
To let history catch its breath.

Long Nights

No place for a final adieu,
No place for sleep – in peace,
Scattered everywhere, only God knows
where,
Present, past and future cut like
undesirable weeds,
All with one savage blow – midstream.

The wounds keep festering like an
infected boil,
To come to a standstill, in blood
drenched territory,
God decided to pitch His tent elsewhere,
Where to administer the final morphine,
in barren territory.

Days have disappeared, shutters are
drawn,
Only night prevails, as a final victor,
Unaware of footsteps on ice, however
hesitantly and slow.

<u>The Well-Meaning</u>

The well-meaning, as we know,
Only show interest and concern,
No other thought crossed their minds,
And this they can vow.

Just like in war,
Territory is invaded,
Armies are set up in a foreign zone,
Air force and navy focus on the foes,
You are lucky if they don't tread on your
toes.

People too can be invaded,
Air and space is taken away,
A take-over bid,
The very lifeline is threatened,
A subtle way of suffocation,
A well-meaning way of manipulation
and strangulation.

The Old Iron

The old-fashioned iron,

Black and glowing,

Loaded with burning coal,

Devoured my white blouse,

Like a demented animal,

It was eaten alive.

Starting with the collar,

Disbelief was an understatement,

The only blouse needed for ceremonial
occasions,

Was singed beyond recognition,

Going up in grey smoke,

Leaving a gaping wound.

Surprise

A time for afternoon resting,
Was not taken lying down.
The audacity of my two year old,
Abandoning her bed, still as a mouse.
No arousal of suspicion.
Confronting us readily dressed and
assembled,
For her afternoon stroll.

Attired, kitted out with coat, bonnet and
basket,
Buttoned and bowed perfectly.
An irresistible challenge.
Total disbelief targeted my orbit.

Falling on Hard Times

Hushed voices, furtive looks,

In a pawn shop.

We bought a selection of rarities for sale,
To be negotiated.

The sympathetic German shopkeeper,
Out of his wits,
To conclude a speedy deal.

Watching the door anxiously,
As if a murderer could break in,
Trading with Jews was not on the
agenda.

The pawnbroker was not aware that he
could ease the stress of life slightly.

Suitcases

My suitcases are always ready for take-
off,
Manifesting themselves like wanderings,
Through the wilderness in ancient times.

Still ready for take-off,
The eternal wandering Jew.

Living here in exile,
Not my homeland.

Always remembering where home is,
Promise not yet fulfilled, full of yearning.

Last time packing in haste,
The only photographs I took – cut
deeply,
How strange, how meaningful.

My mind overflowing with treasures
untold,
Ready to be assembled and evaluated out
of mothballs.

No need to pack,

All is immured in the recesses of my
mind.

It is said,
'Only those who can carry weights
receive packages of unequalled
proportions.'

There is little space for distribution.
So, therein lies the moral.

The Melody

The enchanting melody lingers on,

Evoking dormant memories,

Breaking heart strings,

Conjuring up long shadows.

Fate did not smile at them,

Hope was abundant,

I buried grief,

Surrendering to the melancholic sound,

Being left distraught, inconsolable,

Shattering the well-structured veneer.

'Reflecting the change of time'

Mountains

Feet on the ground,
Peaks heaven bound,
Always striving,
Close to God.

Earthly, level-headed,
Omni-present,
Makes one feel small and modest.
Their scale, great levellers,
A sense of proportion,
Shapes us into dwarves,
From their prospective we are all
miniatures.

Since time immemorial they were there,
And will still be there, after us.

They register silently, Godlike,
overpowering,
Towering above all things, close to God,
They can't be impressed by people.
They are vigilant, having seen it all,
Events are silently registered and
preserved.

Larger than life, what can impress them?
Listen to the unspoken word, it speaks
volumes!
Like mountains.

Daffodils

Since the Dawn of Time,
Pregnant, irrepressible daffodils,
Reclaiming the last territory,
Believing in resurrection.

Their ancestors would be proud of them,
Life pulsating in their veins,
Exhibiting an aura of optimism,
Mesmerising the world with their vivid
colour.

Kew Gardens

Manicured lawns,
Panorama fit for the Garden of Eden.
Ancient trees that have lived through
turbulent centuries,

They have seen it all.
Solitude is their vow,
Not spilling any secrets.

The plants are breathtaking,
They adapt instantly to their
environment.
Their colours and fragrances do not
compete,
All blending into complete harmony.

<u>Old Photographs</u>

Captured in the stillness of time – ready
to be resurrected,
To be recovered and discovered,
To be slotted back in time,
Though before and after time played its
part.

It cannot be dislocated at times and
repaired at will,
It cannot be ignored,
It played its part,
Part of the time.

Old history – for today and tomorrow,
Reflecting the change of time,
And breach of time for always.

Patterns change,
The old world has evaporated,
Worlds revolve like stars in space,
Yet constantly igniting – causing sparks –
like volcanic eruptions.

Pesach

Pesach will never be the same again,
Held in time, only yesterday it seems,
Despite time having cut into time.

Cupboards packed tightly, paper
wrapped,
To separate Pesach dishes.

Every item a collector's item,
New, yet old.

No previous recollection remains,
To identify the well-loved possession.

The whole atmosphere was charged in
mystery,
The spell enveloped our very being.

Father was removed from his own
familiar self,
Spirituality could be touched
everywhere.

Terror enveloped me, it was awe-
inspiring,
Expecting a non-Jewish child,
Hidden under the table,
To support historical evidence.

On just such a Pesach night,
Light and shade swinging between life
and death.

Even now my heart beats, over-reacts,
And captures the unbelievable moment
of eternity.

The enduring legacy.

Memories

Memories fade over years,

The sudden gesture, the sudden smile,

Reveals all there was only to be
rediscovered,

What was always known.

The circuit closes on yesteryear,

The photoscopic lens zooms in on
yesterday,

Held in time and space,

All framed.

Spring Forth

In the autumn of life a breakthrough,
Poems rising from their hibernation,
Emerging rapidly without assistance or
surgery,
Easy labour, no caesarean requiring
anaesthetic.

Perfectly shaped and formed,
A complete delivery, no inducement,
No forceps, no breech,
No drama, no complication,
No post-natal care, no blood transfusion,
An inner urge to see the light of day.

Unexpectedly, yet delayed,
Without medical help at the appointed
time,
A great bonus.

When did conception occur?

Crown Jewels

Standing erect, new sap charging
through veins,

Blossoms erupt in spring of each branch,

Proudly heaven bound like a crown,

Sparkling with diamonds.

Jewels outshining each other,

Captivating the world,

Preparing for a coronation at the
appointed time,

Lit like a candelabra for a festive
occasion.

Humble Mountains

Focused.

Maintaining their unearthly display at
aloofness,

Being close to God and firmaments.

The purity of snow,

Resonating on their peaks.

Undisputed rulers in the stratosphere,

No one to compete with,

A humbling effect on ordinary mortals.

'Dignity'

Away

The remedy – a pre-described
prescription,

Bear it and keep sane,

Sanity for some, poison for others,

Ink on paper is not their only solution,

Keep it at bay; put it under lock and key.

Do not dig it up,

Put it under the carpet.

Look After the Poor

Without fail I took food to a poor family,
There was always enough for the needy,
Not being 'Rothschild's' ourselves it was
no problem.

A joy to behold when entering their
shack,
Like in the play of Tevia the Milkman,
Bringing milk to others,
Eking out their meagre living – happy to
be of service.

Superiority did not invade my being,
Just a daily task, a common occurrence,
More special for a festival or a Shabbat.

The poverty was oppressive, yet the
dignity more so,
Shining through,
'God raises the poor to special heights,
Equal to poor and princes.

Poems

They are all my children,
No one can be singled out above others.

Giving birth was easy, with few
complications,

Having seen the light of day, you're
independent now,

The umbilical cord has been cut,

Like in life, just being is enough,
Establishing your individuality.

You did not ask to be born,
Pressures could not be ignored,

The incubation period was short,
Your foetal position dictated the time,

Luck is needed to become pregnant
unaided,
Without artificial means to carry the full
cycle.

To await the perfect product,
Standing on your own two feet,

To go forth unaided,
To face the unknown.

To expect continuity, to continue,

The creative process is the ultimate,
given to few,

When time is ripe and the mind
receptive,

All in good time.

Erica

You provided shelter when there was
none,
You provided a haven when there was
none,
You provided sunshine when there was
none,
You provided love, trust and loving care
when there was none,
Repairing the un-repairable.

Small in stature, people would not notice
you,
Unmarried, without children,
Except for a devoted brother.

Money was not one of your worldly
possessions,
Luxuries carried no meaning,
But the goodness of your heart knew no
bounds.

The Letter

There was no call,
No letter came,
Time stood still,
Facts Buried,
Covered like solid snow.

Too heavy to shift,
Too late in the day,
Hope appeared without disguise,
To unearth the earthy,
Showing up its treasured possession,
Only to shatter the proof with a kind but
cruel blow.

Retreat to the cover-up,
Retrace its well-trodden path,
Time is standing still,
Better not to have known.

Like a boxer in the ring,
Several blows weaken the system,
Sustained attacks weaken the core,
Defend yourself, conceal the core,
That's the same trick for the boxer and
for me.

Swans

Without preparation for life,
An introduction to life,
Swans know how to instruct their
offspring,
No words are heard,
No manual is read,
Education presents no problem.

Effortlessly they swim along,
Obeying as if by royal command,
Keeping distances, as if measured.

No veering from the path,
All co-ordinated with military precision,
People would envy their discipline,
Truancy is unknown.

How to achieve obedience, by mere
example, baffles the mind,
Delinquency is not known, no need for a
psychoanalyst.

Nothing seems to be on their minds,
Instinct and intuition guide their
behaviour,
Lucky to have escaped the human
predicament.

Does free will play a part?
By honouring their parents,
Are they aware they are obeying the fifth
commandment?

Unable to negotiate a small hill,
Patiently waiting, giving them a chance
again and over again,
To surmount a challenge.

What a Man

My amazing doctor, never giving up,
With a legendary reputation,
Though sparse with words,
Abounding in optimism and hope.

Coming from a dynasty of doctors,
Carrying on the tradition,
Imbued by God and Torah teaching.

No effort was too great,
Every human being counted,
Every problem a challenge,
Unstinting dedication.

His heart in the right place,
With skills to match,
He towers way above others.

His mother worked still in her nineties,
His sons following in his father's path.

Refugees

That's just how it was,
Just like a schtetl,

They brought their baggage along,
A perfect transplant in a foreign land.

They absorbed the good,
Like pawns and weeds,

There was not much choice,
Doors were tightly shut.

Assimilation can be quick or slow,
It's not dictated by self,
But by the world.

Isolation runs counter to progress,

What is progress? Can it be measured?

We all take our history with us,
Wherever we go,

It's the contents that count,
Not the latest fashion.

Acceptance is risky,
Outsiders get no visa,
Hope can get lost.

We were strangers once too – more than
once,

We know how it feels – and how it hurts,

We know all the sensations and pressure
points,

Anaesthesia is not the answer,

Flowers do not survive in the polluted
atmosphere.

Colour

If all the world were the colour white,
There would be no need for whitewash,
Spreading everywhere, beyond its
boundaries,
The colour of pretence.

Black cannot be erased,
It comes through the palette,
To submerge and reject all that has gone
before,
Radically eradicating, blocking out.

We need colours to feel finer shades,
To know the difference between good
and evil,
The canvas has to be invaded and
retouched,
The flag of surrender cannot be accepted.

Sport

Sport was not my favourite pastime,
But Völker ball was hypnotic.
Never missing a ball,
Clasping it close to my chest.
The Olympics did not cater for it.
I would have been a champion.

My opponents were scared of me.
Astounded by my capacity and agility.
Fearless on the pitch.

Hypnotising at all times,
I scored and amazed even myself,
Heralding total disbelief.

<u>A Tribute</u>

Brutality did not brutalise her,
Hardship did not harden her.

Tyranny did not tyrannise her,
Corruption did not corrupt her.

Life has not withered her,
Surviving is not just longevity,
But keeping values intact.

Torture did not betray her trust in others,
Criminality did not incriminate others,

Though small in stature, slight in build,
Her courage is boundless.

Having survived several concentration
camps,
You would imagine her to be a giant.

Her arm imprinted with concentration
camp numbers,

Bear witness to history, never to be erased.

The evidence speaks volumes to generations never to be denied,

Where hope was born in a forgotten planet.

'Letting Go'

What a Loss

Having reached the pinnacle of their
perfection,

The malaise of the crocuses was alarming
though expected,

Blown to the wind,

Awaiting their return another day,

Alarm resonating in their veins,

The colour of their loss,

Was not their true colour.

I Came Alone

No easy option,
Sending your children into the unknown.

They had no life, whilst I had mine,
Resisting being sent away,
To no avail, mother was adamant,
Obeying father's instructions.

Only now realising their colossal wrench,
Appreciating their selfless gesture.

Ignoring the body blows of time,
I feel their pain.

Not unlike Isaac's sacrifice.

Hospital

Inexpertly, to be on the receiving end,
Never a pleasant pastime.

Human frailty surrendering
independence,
At the expense of progress in slow
motion.

Like a record pursuing its own rhythms,
Rotating, moving on relentlessly until the
end,

To a different ethos.

The Rubber Tree

My rubber tree,
Still only a baby,
Received tender loving care,
It thrived on being spoken to,
Never stopped growing in all directions.

Actually taking charge of my place,
Reaching towards the ceiling,
Aiming towards the moon and beyond.

Not expecting such ambitions,
Like having a master over me,
Trying to achieve the impossible without
fail,
Finding a solution was easy, the final end
not so easy,
Taking the pill might have offered a way
out,
Threats fell on deaf ears, how does one
reprimand a truant?
To no avail, the only way out was a
radical gesture.

Throwing him mercilessly into the bin,

By the scruff of his stubborn neck,
Avoiding my eyes to see him broken, his
branches bleeding,
Feeling the white sap spilling out like
blood,
The shock was instant,
He only spread pleasure, I became his
executioner,
I bloodied my hands, ignoring his
pleading while he was bleeding.

Not being a medic I never knew
resurrection was possible,
Except by the grace of God,

We have our limitations,
Or are we equal to God in his handiwork
of days gone by?

We all have our cross to bear – what an
un-Jewish thing to say.

My Cousin's Burial

Standing right in front at the graveside,
Trepidation enveloped me.

Contours of the limp body,
Were visible through the shroud.

The sequence of events was swift,
As if time was not to be lost.

Staring at the depth of the black grave,
It was awesome, worse than the thought
of death.

Hardly space for walking through,
The gravestones were almost greeting
each other.

No space for privacy or contemplation,
You could hear the pervading peace.

Only birds practicing their chorus,
The silence was piercing the air.

Tranquillity transforming the
atmosphere,
Like a lullaby.

I was the only one left in His shrinking
world.

Walking back in silence, our footsteps
echoing,
Over gravelled ground.

Unspoken words told untold stories,
Of memories and more to be cherished.

May God grant her eternal peace.

Numbers

Hands are numbers, days are numbered,
What was the crime?
No justification for such a sentence.

Dressed like clowns,
Due for a circus performance,
It was no laughing matter,
Degradation was a powerful weapon,
Abusive, lowering morale,
Reducing humans to non-entities,
Like crashing a car through a mincing
machine,
Pulverising them to nothing.

Yet spirits survived, not the body,
How much can a human being take
under constant assault?

It happened time and time again,
Spilling blood stains the flesh,
Murdering brutalised on the same level,

Conscience is not affected. Is it
suppressed?
Living with such crimes, surely destroys
individuals totally?
Through depression or excessive guilt,
A prison sentence would not do justice.

Oh God! Pour out thine wroth!
A heavenly earthquake could avenge
such deeds,
Can we ever forgive?
Time has no scale here,
Not now, not in the future,
Will generations be affected?
Signs of some cancers are raising their
ugly head.

Can one measure heart and head?
Will an x-ray determine abnormal genes?
Can laser treatment eradicate pus?
X-rays are not fool-proof, all depends on
interpretations.

Can a U-turn be envisaged?
We cannot provide answers,
Cancer is all pervasive and invasive,
Questions remain, yet cancers spread,
constantly,
Hard to achieve containment.

How could you tolerate destruction of
your greatest creation?
Surrendering your sovereignty on the
sixth day.
Provocation should stir you to a positive
response,
We have been short-changed in the
world of justice,
The way you are looking the other way.

No Forced Entry

Death did not come as a confrontational
agent,
More like a quiet negotiator,
Reasonable but firm, maintaining his
quiet vigil,
Fulfilling his contract, unobtrusively
insisting on his demand.
Maintaining his stance.

Forging his deal, patiently he takes his
time.
Pursuing his object 'till the end.
Throughout the long dark night.

Calmness and peace are his two
companions,
Assisting and creating a heavenly
atmosphere,
I never knew such a quiet entry,
No forcing of doors, no unlocking.
Hoping for such an invasion,
On private property as if the door was
left open for an expectant guest.

Unobserved, making his exit the way he
came,

Leaving no marks, not even a grain of
sand.
Not even a detective would find
fingerprints or evidence of his presence.
Tidings can be good when time is ripe.

Eternal sleep is a bonus in quiet territory,
When the appointment is finally kept,
No brute force.
No terror alarms the deep sleep.

There must be a heaven,
Surrounding heaven and earth to shelter
and care for good people.
They will be in good company,
demanding only the best seats.
We are all coming and going, it is a
question of time,
Our season ticket is one way only.
Return tickets are not issued.

She looked like an angel,
Serene, at peace with herself and the
world,
As if well-prepared.
Why are we scared of death?
I came for her.
She will never know what she did for
me.

Grief

To measure grief, how many tears are
required?
How many gallons of water in the sea?
Obvious questions supplying no obvious
answers,
Hearts can break without breaking sound
barriers.

Tears can be shed, like fountains,
Those who cannot shed tears are at risk,
Tears cannot flow when crystals solidify,
Unblocking drains is risky.

Coming to terms, letting go, moving on,
The usual response,
No learning theory is universal.

All in its own time, as in Kohelet,
Enveloped in their own predicament.

Some put heavy locks on their heart
strings,
Everything is shut off, closed,
People losing keys, the burden too heavy
to bear.

Your lack of size outstripped not only
your stature,
But towered above the tallest people.

A grain of friendship mends broken
vessels,
And in their turn a drop of water
becomes a torrent.

Like glue at its most potent,
You were unaware of your output.

Pity, nobody told you that you were their
anchor.

When all was lost at sea,
The fear of water would hold no
dominion over you.

Postscript

Let them know I have made it,
Almost reaching the end of the road
myself.
A waste of lives cut short in midstream.
Living on borrowed time,
For no substantial gain,
Except for manic calculations,
Satisfying murderous dreams.

Let them know I have made it.
It may ease their pain,
Withdrawing their legacy of guilt.
To put certainty against uncertainty.
Facilitating some peace,
In their unknown resting place.

May the Lord bless thee and keep thee.

'And Finally...'

Graden

Someone called Graden,
Thought he lived in Gan Eden,
But when he matured,
He still was not cured,
Oh – what a leben.

A Man on a Mission

A man was on a mission,
To earn a big commission,
It was not his doing,
By doing the wooing,
It obviously was an omission.

A Bloke with Intention

A bloke had the intention,
To go to some convention,
But when he got there,
The hall was bare,
It obviously was his invention.

Mrs Leven

Mrs Leven,
A brooch on her leiben,
Was sweet, beautiful and neat.
When she was in despair,
She tore out her hair,
And that was the end of her affair.